Overview *Ladybug, Ladybug*

Harry and Holly make ladybugs two ways.

Reading Vocabulary Words
- spots
- leg
- clay

High-Frequency Words
- cut
- for
- goes
- on
- ball
- like
- go
- at

Building Future Vocabulary
* These vocabulary words do not appear in this text. They are provided to develop related oral vocabulary that first appears in future texts.

Words: add — materials — short(s)
Levels: Purple — Orange — Turquoise

Comprehension Strategy
Visualizing information from text, photographs, and diagrams

Fluency Skill
Reading phrases as mini-sentences

Phonics Skill
Demonstrating understanding of possessives (Harry's, Holly's)

Reading-Writing Connection
Listing steps

Home Connection
Send home one of the Flying Colors Take-Home books for children to share with their families.

Differentiated Instructions
Before reading the text, query children to discover their level of understanding of the comprehension strategy — Visualizing information from text, photographs, and diagrams. As you work together, provide additional support to children who show a beginning mastery of the strategy.

Focus on ELL
- Show a picture of a real ladybug. Together point to the features of a ladybug, helping children associate them with correct English terms.

T1

Using This Teaching Version

1. Before Reading

2. During Reading

3. Revisiting the Text

4. Assessment

This Teaching Version will assist you in directing children through the process of reading.

1. **Begin with Before Reading** to familiarize children with the book's content. Select the skills and strategies that meet the needs of your children.

2. **Next, go to During Reading** to help children become familiar with the text, and then to read individually on their own.

3. **Then, go back to Revisiting the Text** and select those specific activities that meet children's needs.

4. **Finally, finish with Assessment** to confirm children are ready to move forward to the next text.

1 Before Reading

Building Background

- Write the word *spots* on the board. Read it aloud. Ask children if they have ever seen the spots on a ladybug. Ask *What color were the ladybug's spots? How big were they? What was the ladybug doing?*

- Introduce the book by reading the title, talking about the cover photograph, and sharing the overview.

Building Future Vocabulary

Use Interactive Modeling Card: Word Map

- Explain that we use *materials* to make things. Write *materials* in the center of the Word Map.

- Ask *What materials do we use to make art?* Fill in the Word Map with children's responses. Ask *Which material is your favorite?*

Introduction to Reading Vocabulary

- On blank cards write: *spots*, *leg*, and *clay*. Read them aloud. Tell children these words will appear in the text of *Ladybug, Ladybug*.

- Use each word in a sentence for understanding.

Introduction to Comprehension Strategy

- Explain that pictures help readers understand words. Sometimes pictures are on the pages of the book. Sometimes readers imagine the pictures in their heads as they read the words.
- Tell children that pictures will help them understand how to make a ladybug.
- Show children the cover of *Ladybug, Ladybug*. Ask *Do you think both ladybugs are made with the same materials?*

Introduction to Phonics

- Write the word **Harry** on the board. Explain that this name belongs to the boy in the book. Write on the board *This is Harry's name.* Read aloud.
- On the board write the names of three children in the class. Beside each name write *This is [child's] name.* Read aloud and point out that you have added *'s* to each name.
- Write the name of another child on the board. Ask *Whose name is this?* When children respond, write *This is [child's] name* on the board, spelling aloud the name and *'s* as you write.

Modeling Fluency

- On the board write: *Ladybug, Ladybug.* Read aloud. Point out Harry's ladybug on the cover and write *Harry's ladybug* on the board.
- Talk about how you pause at the comma in the title but let *Harry's ladybug* flow together.

2 During Reading

Book Talk

Beginning on page T4, use the During Reading notes on the left-hand side to engage children in a book talk. On page 16, follow with Individual Reading.

During Reading

Book Talk

- Ask children to look at the ladybug Harry is holding on the cover and then pick out Harry's ladybug in the photograph on the title page.

- Ask *What do you think Harry's ladybug is made of?* (paper) Ask children to recall and tell about things they have made from paper.

- Ask *Who does the other ladybug belong to?* (It is the girl's ladybug.) *Do you think the book will tell you her name?*

Turn to page 2 — Book Talk

T4

Revisiting the Text

Future Vocabulary
- Ask *What materials did Harry and Holly use to make their ladybugs?* (paper, clay) Talk about the differences in the two ladybugs that result from the materials used.

- Ask *What other materials could Harry and Holly use to make their ladybugs?* (felt, salt dough, papier-mâché)

Now revisit pages 2–3

During Reading

Book Talk

- **Comprehension Strategy** Ask
Do you see Harry's ladybug in the photograph on this page? (no, just the parts of the ladybug) *Can you see a picture in your head of Harry's ladybug when it is all put together?*

- Ask children to refer to their visualizations to predict how the red paper, the black spots, and the two pieces of black paper will come together to make Harry's ladybug.

- Ask children to name the other tools and materials in the photograph and predict how Harry will use them.

Turn to page 4 – Book Talk

Revisiting the Text

Cut the red paper for the ladybug.

Future Vocabulary
- Direct children's attention to all the tools and materials spread out on the table in front of Harry. Ask *Can you think of anything not on the table that Harry needs to make his ladybug?*

- **Comprehension Strategy**
  Encourage children to visualize each step in making Harry's ladybug to see if any needed tools or materials are missing. (Harry has everything he needs on the table.)

Now revisit pages 4–5

During Reading

Book Talk

- **Fluency Skill** Model reading phrases as mini-sentences on these two pages: *The red paper / goes like this. / Cut the legs / for the ladybug.*

- Ask *How is Harry fastening together the cut edges of the red paper?* (with a stapler) Ask children to predict how Harry will fasten the legs to the ladybug's red paper body.

Turn to page 6 — Book Talk

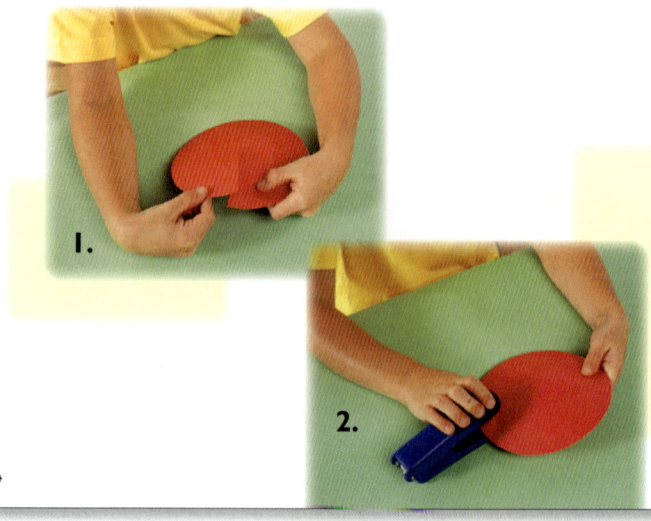

Cut the legs for the ladybug.

Revisiting the Text

Future Vocabulary
- Look at the photograph on page 5. Say *The photograph helps us understand how Harry makes the legs for his ladybug.*
- **Comprehension Strategy** Say *Ladybugs have short legs. What other insects have short legs?* (ants, flies, bees) Encourage children to visualize different insects to help them answer the question.

Now revisit pages 6–7

During Reading

Book Talk

- **Comprehension Strategy** Say *Harry is using glue to fasten the legs to the ladybug. How do you know Harry is using glue?* (The glue stick is shown in the photograph.) Discuss again with children how pictures on the pages of a book help readers understand the words.

- Ask *When Harry gets all the spots on the ladybug, what will still be missing?* (the head and face) Ask children to visualize the finished ladybug in their heads to help them answer the question.

The legs go on the ladybug like this.

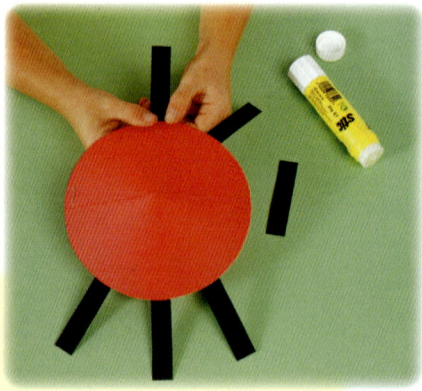

The black spots go on the ladybug like this.

Revisiting the Text

Future Vocabulary

- Have children look at page 6. Ask *How many legs has Harry already added to the ladybug?* (five) *How many are on the table waiting to be added on?* (one) *How many is five added to one?* (six) *Did you know that all insects have six legs?*

- Ask children to name some of the numbers that they can add together.

Now revisit pages 8–9

During Reading

Book Talk

- **Comprehension Strategy** Ask children to close their eyes and see a picture of Harry's ladybug in their head. Ask them to see each part of the ladybug: body, spots, head, and legs. Then have children open their eyes and look again at the photograph of Harry's ladybug. Ask *Was the picture in your head the same as the picture in the book?*

- **Phonics Skill** Ask *Who does the ladybug belong to?* (Harry) Write *Harry* on the board. Say *Yes, it is Harry's ladybug.* Write *Harry's ladybug* on the board and point out that you have added *'s* to show that the ladybug belongs to Harry.

Turn to page 10 – Book Talk

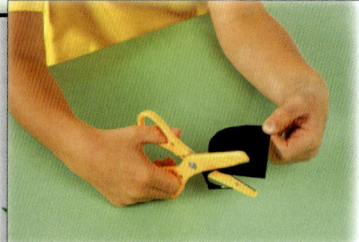

Cut the head for the ladybug.

The head goes on the ladybug like this.

Look at Harry's ladybug.

Revisiting the Text

Future Vocabulary

- Have children look at Harry and Holly in the photograph on page 9. Ask *Who is wearing a shirt with short sleeves?* (Harry) *That's right! Harry is wearing a shirt with short sleeves. Holly's shirt has long sleeves.*

- Ask *Can you tell from the picture if Harry and Holly are wearing shorts?* (no) Talk to children about the kind of weather in which Harry and Holly might wear shorts.

Now revisit pages 10–11

During Reading

Book Talk

- Say *Now you know the girl's name! What is it?* (Holly)

- **Comprehension Strategy** Ask *Do you see Holly's ladybug in the pictures on these two pages?* (no, just red clay and black clay) Ask children to close their eyes and try to visualize Holly's ladybug that they saw earlier on the cover and title page of the book.

- Ask *How is Holly making the red clay into the shape of a ladybug?* (pressing with her hands) Ask children to recall and describe when they have made things out of clay. Ask them if they think Holly will use a stapler or a glue stick to hold together the parts of her ladybug.

Turn to page 12 — Book Talk

10

Here is a ball of red clay.

The red clay goes like this.

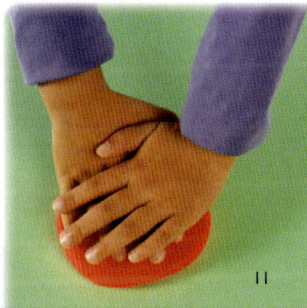

Revisiting the Text

Future Vocabulary
- Look again at the photograph on page 10 and point out the black clay and red clay on the table. Ask *Does Holly have all the materials she needs to make her ladybug?* (yes)

- Ask *Which of these materials will Holly use to make her ladybug's head?* (black clay) *Which of these materials will she use to make her ladybug's little spots?* (black clay)

Now revisit pages 12–13

During Reading

Book Talk
- Ask children to look at the two photographs on pages 12 and 13. Ask *Do these pictures help you understand how Holly is making her ladybug's legs?* (She is rolling each leg with her hand.)

- **Comprehension Strategy** Say *It looks like she is putting each leg into a hole in the piece of red clay.* Ask children to close their eyes and visualize how Holly might have made the holes. Then have them open their eyes. Ask *How do you think she made the little holes in the red clay?* (She might have used her finger or a pencil to poke the holes.)

Turn to page 14 – Book Talk

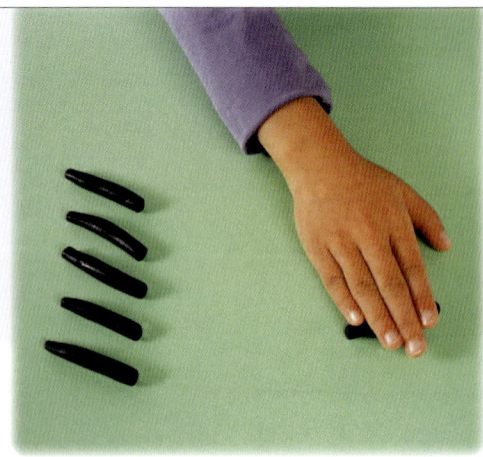

Here are the legs for the ladybug.

The legs go on the ladybug like this.

Revisiting the Text

Future Vocabulary
- Say *Harry and Holly add things to the round body part to make their ladybugs. What other animals could they make by adding things to the round body part?* (spider, beetle, turtle, porcupine)

Now revisit pages 14–15

During Reading

Book Talk
- **Fluency Skill** Model reading phrases as mini-sentences on pages 14 and 15: *Here are / the little spots / for the ladybug. / The head goes / on the ladybug / like this.*

Turn to page 16 – Book Talk

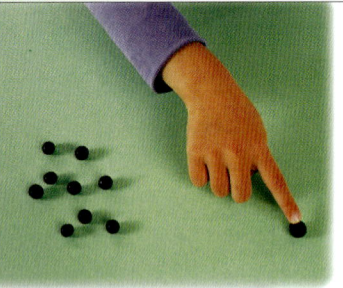

Here are the little spots for the ladybug.

The little spots go on the ladybug like this.

Here is the head for the ladybug.

The head goes on the ladybug like this.

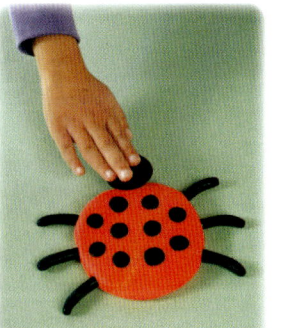

Revisiting the Text

Future Vocabulary
- Have children look at the photographs on pages 14 and 15. Ask *How many spots did Holly add to her ladybug?* (ten) *How many legs did she add?* (six) *How many heads did she add?* (one) Write the three numbers in a column on the board.

- *Can you add the numbers together? How many parts did Holly add to her ladybug altogether?* (seventeen)

Go to page T5 – Revisiting the Text

During Reading

Book Talk
- Leave this page for children to discover on their own when they read the book individually.

Individual Reading
Have each child read the entire book at his or her own pace while remaining in the group.

Go to page T5 – Revisiting the Text

Look at Holly's ladybug.

During independent work time, children can read the online book at:
www.rigbyflyingcolors.com

16

Revisiting the Text

Future Vocabulary
- Use the notes on the right-hand pages to develop oral vocabulary that goes beyond the text. These vocabulary words first appear in future texts. These words are: *add*, *materials*, and *short(s)*.

Turn back to page 1

Reading Vocabulary Review
Activity Sheet: Word Sorter

- Ask children to write these words in the correct spaces of the Word Sorter: *clay, red clay, black clay, legs, spots, head,* and *body.*
- Ask children to think of two more things that could be made from red clay and to write them in the remaining level-three spaces.

Comprehension Strategy Review
Use Interactive Modeling Card: Summarizing

- Tell children that readers often take notes for a text to help them remember or find information.
- Together fill in the Summarizing chart for *Ladybug, Ladybug,* using page spread numbers and descriptive words and short phrases.

Phonics Review
- Have children look for the possessive forms of *Harry* and *Holly.* (pp. 2, 9, 10, 16)
- Ask children to use the words *Harry's* and *Holly's* aloud in sentences.

Fluency Review
- Write phrases from several of the book's sentences on strips of paper. Use the strips to demonstrate how good readers read in clumps of words rather than word by word. For example: *Cut the legs / for the ladybug.*
- Hold up strips one at a time so that children may practice phrasing before reading a sentence in its entirety.

Reading-Writing Connection
Activity Sheet: Summarizing Chart

To assist children with linking reading and writing:
- Review steps for making a ladybug and write the list on the board: gathering materials; forming the red body; adding on the legs, spots, and head.
- Have children complete the Summarizing Chart using the list.

T5

4 Assessment

Assessing Future Vocabulary

Work with each child individually. Ask questions that elicit each child's understanding of the Future Vocabulary words. Note each child's responses:

- If you could add one thing to your lunch today, what would it be?
- What materials are needed to build a campfire?
- Can you think of something you are too short to reach? What?

Assessing Comprehension Strategy

Work with each child individually. Note each child's understanding of visualizing information from text, photographs, and diagrams:

- What did Holly look like? What was she wearing? How do you know?
- What things were on Harry's table before he started making his ladybug? How do you know?
- Did Harry have to cut out each of the black spots for his ladybug? How do you know?
- Show me how Holly made the legs for her ladybug. How do you know she did it this way?

Assessing Phonics

Work with each child individually. Have each child use a card and marker to make a label for one item in the classroom, using the possessive form, such as *Bill's backpack.* Ask *Whose backpack is it?* (Bill's) Note each child's responses for understanding possessives:

- Did each child correctly add the *'s* to the written name?
- Did each child voice the *'s* when using the possessive form aloud?

Assessing Fluency

Have each child read one sentence of the text aloud to you in turn. (You may read pages 2 and 10.) Note each child's understanding of reading phrases as mini-sentences:

- Did each child say one word at a time, or did he or she read words in clusters?
- Were junctures between phrases arbitrary or in keeping with sentence meaning and structure?
- Did each child use tone of voice to reinforce phrasing?

Interactive Modeling Cards

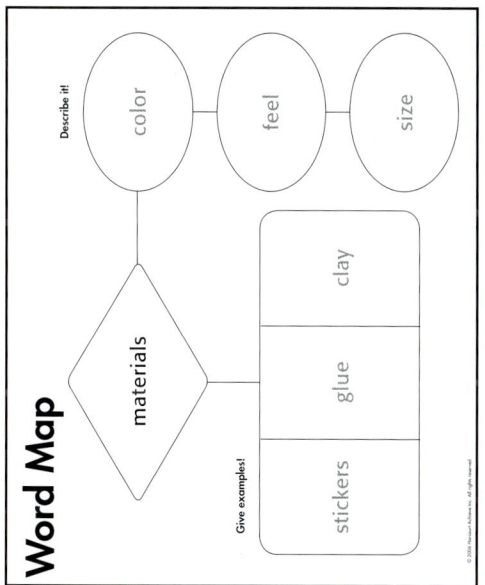

Summarizing

Page	Summary
2–3	Harry's ladybug, paper
4–5	body, legs
6–7	legs, spots
8–9	head, done
10–11	Holly's ladybug, clay
12–13	legs
14–15	spots, head
16	done

Directions: With children, fill in the Word Map using the word *materials*.

Directions: With children, fill in the Summarizing chart for *Ladybug, Ladybug.*

Discussion Questions

- How many legs did Holly add to her ladybug? (Literal)
- How is the face on Harry's ladybug different from the face on Holly's ladybug? (Critical Thinking)
- Do you think it is easier to make a paper ladybug or a clay ladybug? Why? (Inferential)

Activity Sheets

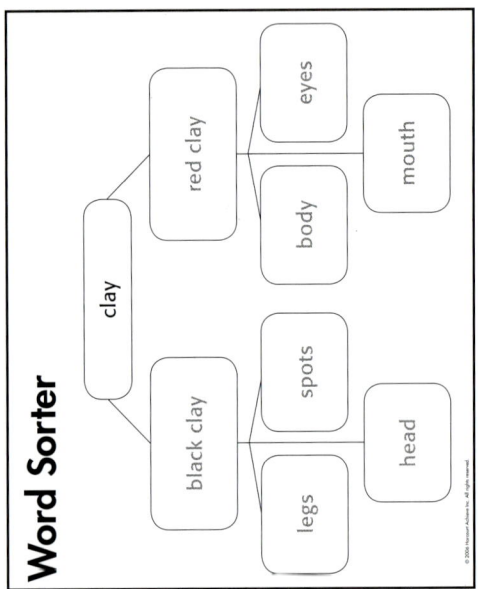

Directions: Have children fill in the Word Sorter using the word *clay* in the top space.

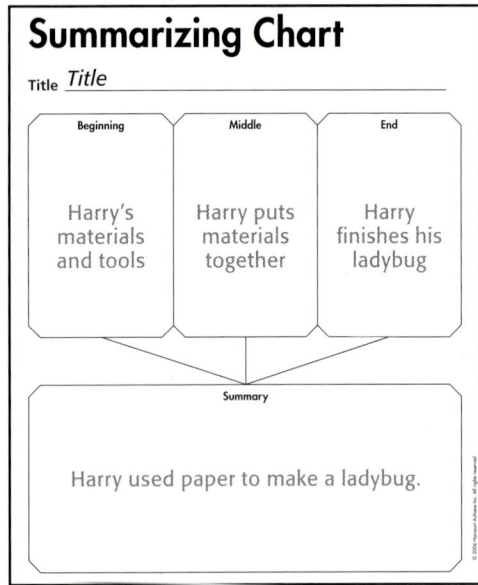

Directions: Have children fill in the Summarizing Chart with the steps for making either Harry's or Holly's ladybug.